It's Time

My Journey to Purpose

Meagan Pinkney

It's Time : My Journey to Purpose
Copyright © 2022 by Meagan Pinkney

ISBN: 978-0-9971852-6-3 (ebook)
ISBN: 978-0-9971852-7-0 (paperback)

Published by: Joseph's Ministry, LLC
www.josephsministryllc.com

Cover design by Ramond Walker at Walker Legacy
http://www.walkerlegacy.co/

Scripture quotations marked NIV are taken from The Holy Bible, New International Version®, NIV® Copyright 1973, 1978, 1984, 2011 by Biblica, Inc.TM Used by Permission. All rights reserved worldwide.

Scripture quotations marked NLT are taken from the Holy Bible, New Living Translation, copyright 1996, 2004, 2007, 2015 by Tyndale House Foundation. Used by permission of Tyndale House Publishers, Inc., Carol Stream, Illinois 60188. All rights reserved.

Scripture quotations marked (ESV) are taken from THE HOLY BIBLE, ENGLISH STANDARD VERSION®, Copyright© 2001 by Crossway, a publishing ministry of Good News Publishers. Used by permission.

All rights reserved. Printed in the United States of America. No part of this book may be used or reproduced in any manner whatsoever without written permission from the author except in the case of brief quotations embodied in critical articles or reviews.

CONTENTS

Dedication i

Introduction 1

Chapter 1: And So It Begins 7

Chapter 2: God is Sovereign 13

Chapter 3: Trust God 21

Chapter 4: It's God, Not You 27

About the Author 33

Dedication

First, I want to thank God the Father, Son, and the Holy Spirit for empowering me on my journey to purpose. Without your love and power, there is no testimony to share for overcoming.

I wrote this book to enlighten everyone on their journey to never give up on their God-given dreams. The Lord has heard your distress call and has sent my testaments in this book to help guide you through the delivery process successfully, like the role of a midwife. So be encouraged and get ready to push because IT'S TIME!

Meagan Pinkney

Introduction

PUSH! KEEP BREATHING! YOU ARE DOING GREAT! Do these phrases sound familiar? Of course, they do! They are just a few expressions that you should expect to hear in a labor or delivery room. As you know, nine months or 39 weeks is the timeframe for a baby to develop fully in a mother's womb. It is a process. However, did you know you are in the midst of your own process? Your process may not involve delivering a physical human being, BUT I have come to enlighten you that you are being prepared to birth something great, much greater, in your life!

For all to be well with the baby on this side of the mother's womb, every step must be complete before the delivery phase can occur. It is a process. In your life, you must come to an internal place of being okay with the process, your process. Knowing and understanding that your process will NOT be a smooth ride is essential. What if I guaranteed you that the process would not be smooth at all but a messy one? What if I told you that your process could not be skipped? Like the child in the mother's womb, the process is where the vital developmental stages occur for the child. Such as, the child's arms and legs are formed, the brain is developed, the skin is produced, the gender is determined and revealed, and so on. I believe you would agree that the development of the child's arms, legs, brain, and gender is vital to the child's life function.

I must be transparent and say something that may shock you, but it is true – (raising my right hand) I, Meagan Pinkney, do not like the process and have been caught praying to God that He speeds up my process to reach the result/promised land quicker! In other words, I am asking God, the creator of all things, if I could skip some steps in my process. Can you relate?

Thinking to yourself, Surely the grass is greener on the "other side." But we must be careful what we ask for or even think.

Concerning the child in the womb, we are saying, Lord, I know you have plans for my arms to develop and grow during this part of my process, but do I need my arms? We can skip that step. Yeah, Lord, about those legs, I was thinking that I could figure out how to walk without my legs later. Let's keep this train moving forward – all aboard!

This mindset reminds me of what is recorded in Exodus 13:17 NIV. This scripture says, "When Pharaoh let the people go, God did not lead them on the road through the Philistine country, though that was shorter. God said, "If they face war, they might change their minds and return to Egypt." Verse 18 continues, saying, "So God led the people around by the desert road toward the Red Sea. The Israelites went up out of Egypt ready for battle." This situation shows me that God knew His people and what they did and did not need to reach AND occupy the promised land successfully. It is a process.

Oh, so you can not relate to the baby analogy, you say. No problem, I got you! You may say, Lord, I do not need to know this man or woman fully before marriage. Let's move forward because I am getting older, and my clock keeps ticking. Or, Lord, I do not have that much time in my day to spend with you and get to know you for myself. So, I will take the Pastor's word for it and shout and act a fool at church so that people will think I am more spiritual than I am. It is a process.

I was told skipping steps is like taking a toll road versus the main overpopulated busy highway. Yes, you get to your destination quicker, but you will have to pay for it somewhere down the road! It's time for the Body of Christ to realize that everything you have been through up to this point in your life has been the development phase for what is to come afterward. God has intentions for your life, no matter how old or young you are.

"For I know the plans I have for you," says the LORD. "They are plans for good and not for disaster, to give you a future and a hope." Jeremiah 29:11 NIV

NOW is the time to birth what the Lord has placed on the inside of you to bless your world and advance the Kingdom of God! These are the end times, and I believe the Lord is saying to us today, It's Time;

your water just broke! The following chapters are a few points I want to share with you to help you prepare for giving birth in this season of your life.

And So It Begins 1

And so, it begins! Often, the question asked is, *what is your purpose?* This question can be very intimidating to people. Instead of asking the question, *what is your purpose?* Consider asking; *you know you have a unique purpose, right?* The reason that you were born. The reason that you were born the race you were, into the family you were, in the country that you were, and the gender that you were. There is a purpose for it all. I like to think about purpose like this - I was in God's thoughts before I was physically born into the Earth (according to Jeremiah 1:5 NIV). God knows the end from the beginning and foreknew that He needed a solution on Earth to solve a particular problem. Because He knew me, He chose me to be the vessel He would use on Earth to be the solution when it was time. I am on this Earth on purpose for a purpose.

Over the years, I have come to believe that every lesson, victory, failure, and everything in between was preparation to get me prepared for something greater. Something greater is coming to those that have accepted Jesus Christ into their hearts and have yielded their lives to His leading. If you still need to, there is still time! I have included a salvation prayer at the end of this chapter, especially for you. God desires for His children to know Him and be saved. God needs you to introduce the entire world to Jesus Christ. Yes, you are to be a willing vessel for Him to use. You have a purpose.

People need you, the real you, the authentic you, to show up. People are waiting on you! I believe that certain people are assigned to our lives, and if we do not show up or get over ourselves, those people will miss a unique piece of God's expression on Earth. God's love and power can only be displayed through you. **It's Time.** People are waiting on you. Someone told me years ago sometimes people feel that they can not move forward until someone they admire or look up to permits them to do so. Well, I am permitting you to move out of your comfort zone, accept Jesus Christ into your heart and life, seek Him for purpose and walk in your purpose like never before. That is, being scared and all.

For me, I have always felt that there was more. More to life, more to *my* life. As a young girl, I began having dreams of things that would eventually come to pass in my life. I would later record my dreams in my journal, along with the date that I received the dream. The more I sought God and inquired about my specific purpose, the more dreams I would have. God spoke to me in the night season through my dreams like He often would to several individuals in the Bible. One dream that I received back in January 2014 is recorded in my journal as the following:

> *"I had a dream that I was getting married, and I arrived at the church very early on my wedding day. However, when I arrived, there were people at the church already, but it was crazy. Several people at the church were pregnant, and they all went into labor at the church simultaneously. I was doing all the work by myself. I was so tired, but I managed. I was able to 'deliver' all these babies before the wedding started."*

Once I received this dream, I had no clue of its meaning. Finally, after praying and asking the Holy Spirit for the interpretation of the meaning, I received the following meaning:

"I believe that the Lord would use me to assist individuals to give birth to their dreams and promises from God in the midst of God birthing my dreams and promises."

Later that year, in October 2014, I officially established my business Joseph's Ministry, LLC, as directed by the Holy Spirit. Not even considering my dream, I moved forward with launching my business and helping others give birth to those long-awaited dreams and things that God placed in their hearts. God made me the solution (my company) to a problem that I did not know existed, but He foreknew it. After a year of being a business owner, the Holy Spirit reminded me of the dream He gave me about delivering many babies. Wow! I love the way that God chooses to speak to us. I am confident that I am walking in the perfect will of God and His purpose for my life in this area. My business has received numerous testaments from our clients about the timeliness of my business being established, the name of my company, and the services we provide. To God be the glory!

Even as the business clients were giving birth to their dreams through my business, I, too, was giving birth. The process was messy at times, challenging, exhausting, frustrating, and rewarding all at the same time. Had I skipped steps in my personal journey, this business, my baby, would be lacking in a few areas. Just like parenthood, your children teach you a lot about yourself. I have birthed patience, character, integrity, and another level of seeking God's presence. But imagine, what if my business never showed up to the scene? What if I never intentionally began to seek God for His purpose in my life? What would happen to the people sent to my business and the many more coming? These are the exact thoughts that continue to ignite my seek for God. Some people call me a purpose pusher. We should all be purpose pushers for each other. I want to avoid being the hold-up for someone fully walking into their next level of purpose or vice versa. **It's Time.**

There comes a time when the doctor and nurses proclaim to the mother that it's time to deliver. I believe this is your time. Consider me your midwife as we move along this birthing process. We are all in this process together. Through the pain and heavy breathing, try focusing on the reward of your labor, the baby. Your purpose, which is your baby, is essential and needed on Earth. My suggestion at this point is to assume the birthing position and push! **It's Time.**

Salvation Prayer

Dear heavenly Father, thank you for loving me and seeing me. Thank you for sending your son Jesus Christ to die on the cross for my sins. Please forgive me. I am now ready to be saved. I openly declare, according to your word in Romans 10:9-10 that Jesus is Lord, and I believe in my heart that God raised him from the dead. And with my declaration, I am saved by faith. In Jesus' name. Amen.

God is Sovereign 2

My first point of wisdom to help you prepare for your birthing season is to know that **God is sovereign**. The word sovereign describes God's supreme rulership in our lives.[1] He controls everything! When I say everything, this means everything. The sovereignty of God may be a new word or concept to most people; however, once introduced to it, things change. Your way of thinking about God and your life changes. Sometimes, I must admit that I think I am in control of my life. Then the Lord brings me into a situation

---

[1] Oxford Languages. (n.d.). *Oxford English Dictionary*, December 19, 2022, from https://www.google.com/search?q=sovereign&oq=sovereign&aqs=chrome..69i57j0i433i5 12l4j0i512j46i131i433i512j0i512j0i433i512l2.215j0j15&sourceid=chrome&ie=UTF-8

that quickly shows my dependency on Him and Him alone. We are not "in control" of anything. Therefore, when we pray, we should be confident that nothing is too small or too big for our God to handle. **God is sovereign.** During your birthing season, reading and studying the word of God is vital to the transition. When pressure arrives (and it will), you must know that God is the King of kings and Lord of lords in our situations. As days go by and you do not know if you are coming or going, who's your friend or friendenemy, you must know and be sure that God is in control of the wind, rain, and sunshine in your life. God controls everything and is over everything!

To break this point down even further, think of at least one person you know who has authority in your life. A Pastor, the President, a manager, a leader, or maybe even yourself. The person that you correct your posture for when they walk into a room, the person that you try to impress with your good works, the person that you change your entire wardrobe to come up to their level, that person. Well, did you know that God has rulership over that person? But we (yes, we) do not do nearly half of the life changes we make for a man to give honor and respect to God. He *is* the ultimate ruler over everything that is created. Nothing and no one rules over God. Everything starts and stops with Him. We serve, pray to, and worship this true and living God. **God is sovereign.**

> *"—he who is the blessed and only Sovereign, the King of kings and Lord of lords," 1 Timothy 6:15 ESV*

With His sovereign purpose for our lives, God uses His providence to move us, arrange things in our lives, and change our situations and circumstances to fulfill this sovereign purpose. Although we all have free will, I believe the explanation that Pastor/Teacher Tony Evans says best is "that even our free will does not fall outside of the boundaries of God's sovereignty." Wow, that is pretty awesome! Why do you think Romans 8:28 is even possible? This scripture reads, "And we know that God *causes* everything to work together for the good of those who love God and are called according to His purpose for them." HE IS THE SOVEREIGN LORD, AND BESIDES HIM, THERE IS NO OTHER. Acknowledging Him as the sovereign Lord puts things back into perspective. By doing this, we put Him back on the throne of our lives. God is NOT Santa Clause. He is also NOT some guy you occasionally talk to and see from up the street! My Bible tells me that He is the same God yesterday, today, and forever.

"Jesus Christ is the same yesterday, today, and forever."

Hebrews 13:8 NIV

He is the SAME God that walked with Adam in the cool of the day (Genesis 3:8 NIV), the SAME God who called out to Moses from the burning bush (Exodus 3:2 NIV), the SAME God that split the Red Sea and allowed the Israelites to walk across on dry land (Exodus 14:22 NIV), and the SAME God who commissioned Joshua and told him to be strong and courageous to be able to lead the people into the promised land (Deuteronomy 31:7 NIV)! This is the SAME sovereign God who we worship today! Thank God that although people change, He never changes.

Providence Example

If you are anything like me, I need examples to follow along and comprehend some things. I wanted to practically share a personal example of God's sovereignty, specifically His providence, with you for better understanding. In my book, "By Faith: My Journey of Obedience," I shared my testimony of suddenly quitting my Engineering job to follow Jesus. My reason for leaving was NOT my idea nor a part of MY plan. Nearing the end of a 21-day fast, I knew that the Holy Spirit was asking me to quit my job, so, by faith, I left. During those "wilderness years," I found myself having a front-row seat to witness God's providence personally.

After an adventurous year and a half, the Lord did exactly what He said He would do; have me return to Engineering. Seemingly out of nowhere, I received an email from a recruiter about an Engineering position with a local company for a 6-month contract. I was hired for this contract position and later transitioned as a full-time Engineer at that facility. I was employed with this company for six months before they laid everybody in the office off and closed the shop! In the natural, this situation sounds devasting, but it was all planned under God's providence. Thinking back on this experience, it was indeed God's love and grace this all happened. God knew the layoff was coming and protected me financially by causing me to find favor with my manager and the company offering me the full-time position. Therefore, when the layoffs occurred, I was eligible for the severance package as a full-time employee versus not receiving anything being only a contract employee. God is sovereign, and His providential work is active in our lives.

Although I was laid off from one company, the Lord already had *MY* new position saved and ready for me. You see, at the same time the layoff was occurring, the Lord had opened a door at the company He told me to quit. I was favored to accept the SAME Engineering position I quit, same salary, and the company awarded me my previous service years back! This means, on paper, that I never left the company. To God be the glory!! I genuinely hope you see God's masterful hand in all the details! I am a detail person, and I love that I serve the God that delights in the details of our lives!

"The LORD directs the steps of the godly. He delights in every detail of their lives." Psalms 37:23 NLT

To read more details about my faith experience, purchase the book today! It will indeed bless you and challenge you to seek God, hear His voice, obey Him and do it all by faith!

Trust God — 3

Now that we understand the meaning of God's sovereignty, my next point of wisdom is to **trust God**. When God is getting ready to birth through your life, we must put our FULL trust in Him. Now, this point can trip you up if you are not careful. I trust God. I must trust God. I will trust God. I trust God. It was effortless for me to say aloud or even type those words in this book. However, when everything comes to light, and you have to walk out your faith daily and continue trusting God, it is not that easy. It is now time to trust God *for* everything and *with* everything.

You must know that you know, that you know, that God is real and that He will never leave or forsake you. Ever.

"For God has said, "I will never fail you. I will never abandon you."" Hebrews 13:5 NLT

We must trust that God is who He says He is. Things are getting darker and darker in this world; therefore, we can not go by what things look like with our natural eyes to determine if things are okay. No! The Word of God says that the just shall live by faith! We must seek God's face and read His word daily for Him to guide and direct our lives. These are the end times, and God's people need to know that God is saying, **"It's time; I have prepared you for this, it's time."**

Trust and Faith Example

As I stated in the providence example, I want to share that same example from a different perspective. My life, at that time, was calm and less 'interrupted' when the divine invitation came to me during my time of fasting to leave my job to follow God. Now, there were several potential problems with this request:

1. How was I going to get money?

2. Where am I following you too?

None of these questions or concerns of mine were answered by the Holy Spirit, but I *decided* to step out on faith and trust God's leading. This leading was indeed another level of trust in God's word for me. So, for one year and several months, I found myself on this journey of trusting God. God designed this stage in my process to strip away my old mindset of God and how He provides for our daily needs.

This step of trusting God alone to provide for me was pretty daunting. I have always considered myself a good steward of my finances and was thankful for my good-paying career. But something crept into my heart over the years that I did not realize, pride. Yes, I knew the Lord gave me my job, and I acknowledged that often. However, my dependence on my consistent paycheck replaced my dependence on God as my provider. So obeying God to trust Him fully to be my provider was indeed a gift from God. I have heard the saying; how will we know that God is Jehovah Jireh (the Lord will provide) if we are never in a situation where we need Him to be the provider? How will we know that God is Jehovah Shalom (the Lord is peace) if we never need peace? How will we know that God is Jehovah Rapha (the Lord that heals) if we never needed healing?

During this time, I traveled as I had never traveled before in assisting a traveling Evangelism ministry, hosted my first book tour, completed my first speaking engagement, and so on. But as quickly as that journey started was as soon as that journey came to an end. The sovereign God sent me back to work. For the entire time, I lacked for nothing! If I was short on a bill, the Lord would have someone put money into my hands. Talk about the next level of trusting God! I also learned several scriptures and had them in a chokehold because they were all I was holding. Thank God that His word did not return to Him void! Say aloud in your atmosphere – I WILL **TRUST GOD**!!

"Blessed is the man who trusts in the LORD, whose trust is the LORD." Jeremiah 17:7 NIV

In your birthing season, trusting God will become your foundation and launching pad for situations that will appear in the seasons to come. As important as it is for mothers to set the foundation of healthy living for their growing fetus before birth. The second season of your life will thank you for setting a proper foundation now. Being firmly planted in the word of God and your trust and belief in God's character will sustain you for the rest of your life.

It is essential to know that trusting God does not apply only to the big things that God may ask us to do. Trusting God also applies to your family, money stewardship, health, career, and education. During my trusting example, I remember being in the middle of it all and asking God not to let me forget this practice of seeking Him and trusting Him for e-v-e-r-y-t-h-i-n-g. Since returning to my career and starting my own business, I honestly seek God and trust God for everything. Because *now* I *know* where my help comes from and where my source is. Knowing still does not make the process easy, but it does invite comfort and peace along the journey with you. So trust the great physician to guide you through your birthing season successfully.

It's God, Not You   4

The third wisdom point to remember is that God is doing the work, not you. Not to take away from your *awesomeness* but what will be produced through you is not because of you. This is the point that keeps you humble and honest. God wants, gets, and deserves *all* of the glory from our lives. We do not deserve to be used in the way He is getting us prepared through the wisdom shared in this book. God is a gracious God. He chooses to use His created beings on this Earth to advance His kingdom. God is trusting us to give Him all the glory. We must ensure that everything points back to Him. If He has given you the desire to write a book, it's for His glory. If you desire to start a business, it's for His glory. Produce a movie, yep, all for His glory! We can not honestly believe that we have been that good to deserve the many blessings God bestows upon us. **It's God, not you.** Active humility is critical to God continuing to use us as we move forward to Harvest time. The word humility can be described as a modest or low view of one's importance or humbleness.[2] As we humble ourselves before God daily, He will forever reign. Now is not the time to question your allegiance to God. God has been and still is very good to His children. If you need further convincing, I challenge you to look back over your life and remember the many ways God made for you, your family, and your friends. God desires to use each one of us but taking His glory is a no-go. God shares His glory with no one. If you are curious to see what happens if one tries to take or even think about sharing the glory with God, I invite you to read the fall of Lucifer in Isaiah 14. As God begins using you in miraculous

---

[2] Oxford Languages. (n.d.). *Oxford English Dictionary*, December 19, 2022, from https://www.google.com/search?q=humility&biw=1158&bih=724&sxsrf=ALiCzsakF70Oq0Io2uUDD7fnc3pbl4wkew%3A1671477398005&ei=lbigY6T8PMyn_QaAl4foCg&ved=0ahUKEwjkmrvEsob8AhXMU98KHYDLAa0Q4dUDCBE&uact=5&oq=humility&gs_lcp=Cgxnd3Mtd2l6LXNlcnAQAzIKCAAQRxDWBBCwAzIKCAAQRxDWBBCwAzIKCAAQRxDWBBCwAzIKCAAQRxDWBBCwAzIKCAAQRxDWBBCwAzIKCAAQRxDWBBCwAzIKCAAQRxDWBBCwAzIHCAAQsAMQQzIHCAAQsAMQQzIHCAAQsAMQQzIHCAAQsAMQQzINCAAQ5AIQ1gQQsAMYATINCAAQ5AIQ1gQQsAMYATIPCC4Q1AIQyAMQsAMQQxgCMhUILhDHARDRAxDUAhDIAxCwAxBDGAIyDwguENQCEMgDELADEEMYAkoECEEYAEoECEYYAVAAWABgmAJoAXABeACAAQCIAQCSAQCYAQDIARLAAQHaAQYIARABGAnaAQYIAhABGAg&sclient=gws-wiz-serp

ways, remain humble. When the sick become healed, remain humble. When the blind begin to see, remain humble. When evil spirits are cast out, and deliverance takes place, remain humble. **It's God, not you.**

"If my people, who are called by my name, will humble themselves and pray and seek my face and turn from their wicked ways, then I will hear from heaven, and I will forgive their sin and will heal their land." 2 Chronicles 7:14 NIV

The word of God says that God does what pleases Him! He is sovereign. He shows mercy to whom He shows mercy, and he does have plans for your life, according to Jeremiah 29:11 NIV. This scripture is my life scripture because years ago, when I first started seeking God for real, I would sit quietly in my house and listen to hear anything from God. And one day, I heard an audible voice say, "I know the plans I have for you." I did not know that was a scripture at that time, so I grabbed my phone and googled those words. And today, I believe the Holy Spirit is saying those exact words to those reading this book. I know the plans I have for your life, and now is the time for those plans to be made known to the world for my glory! Now is the time for you to step out on faith. Now is the time to start that business, write that book, and accept your calling into ministry. Now! Now is the time. And the Lord says, no longer will my words be delayed!

Church, get ready for a move of God in and through your life. I declare Isaiah 61 over you right now. That the Spirit of the Sovereign Lord is upon you...

because the Lord has anointed me

to proclaim good news to the poor.

He has sent me to bind up the brokenhearted,

to proclaim freedom for the captives

and release from darkness for the prisoners,

Today I proclaim this is the year of the Lord's favor for your life. **It's Time!**

Let us Pray

Father, in the name of Jesus, sweep through the place where the person reading this book is and in your people's hearts and minds. Remove all doubt, fear, and confusion, and fill us afresh and anew with your Holy Spirit and love overflowing. I pray that your fire burns up every impurity and that our faith will be proven genuine and pleasing in your sight. I pray for your wind to blow in our lives and the atmosphere and for those that receive your words will receive the gift of the Holy Spirit with the evidence of speaking in tongues. Do a new thing inside of us today. Now Lord, now! For your glory! In Jesus' name, we pray, amen!

About the Author

Meagan Pinkney is a speaker, best-selling author, minister, and entrepreneur. She is the author of Waiting While You Wait, Pray Eat Lift, By Faith, and contributing author of Inner Circle and Daily Dose of Declarations. Using her life as an example, Meagan is focused on showing others that there is great value inside them waiting to be birthed into the Earth. This is the message that Meagan is sharing with individuals everywhere that she goes. She believes that NOW is the time for your purpose to be revealed and manifested through your life for the glory of God.

www.meaganpinkney.com

PUBLISHED MATERIAL BY MEAGAN PINKNEY

Waiting While You Wait: My Journey Through Singleness

In this book, I will share several personal testimonies from my journey as a single woman as I have learned to wait on God. When an individual yields them self to the Holy Spirit, for the use of the Kingdom, you will be amazed by the testimonies you will be able to share. Instead of me forgetting all the wonderful, supernatural things God has done in and through my life, I wanted to write all of them down to pass on to other Believers, especially those who are currently single. I believe it is an extremely important task to pass on to others what God can and will do for us if we learn to wait on Him (like a waiter) while we are in the process of waiting (for the purpose)! The purpose of this book is to motivate individuals to lean on God for everything, whether big or small. God loves us dearly and He wants to see us prosper. Singles should know that singleness is a beautiful thing and should definitely be valued as it is a blessing from God- whether you are single for a season or a lifetime.

Pray Eat Lift: My Journey Through Weightloss

In today's society, everyone wants to know how to lose weight instantly. Some recommendations are to explore those celebrity and military diets or just simply not eating. To be honest, if this could be done everyone would do it…right? Being conscious of our weight or waistline is something that a majority of people can relate to. According to the Centers for Disease Control and Prevention (CDC), more than one-third (34.9% or 78.6 million) of U.S. adults are obese. I can only speak for myself that I do not want to be included in that 34.9%, but in reality I was stuck there for several years of my young life until something changed! In this book, I will share my personal testimony of my supernatural weight loss journey. My journey, although quite unique, will encourage you and hopefully kick-start your own personal weight loss journey and relationship with the Holy Spirit. Whether we realize it or not the excess weight that we are physically carrying around is a huge hindrance to our productiveness in life. Once we can develop a healthy balance of praying, eating and lifting then our journey can begin.

By Faith: My Journey of Obedience

"Are you willing to use your life for a greater purpose? I understand that this is not the most popular thing to do in this age, but what if you allowed God to use your life in unorthodox ways to show the world His goodness, love, mercy, favor and that He really does exist? "YES, of course," you may say! But are you willing to pay the cost to intimately pursue this lifestyle? In this book, I will tell you about my powerful journey of obedience, sharing real life examples of what it looks like to hear and obey the Holy Spirit, make mistakes, and do it all by faith. My testimony will surely bless your life and change your perspective of what it means to follow Christ…today."

Inner Circle: One God Three Friends

This book will display the journey of one God and three women earnestly seeking God's perfect will in their lives. With the leading of the Holy Spirit, we stepped out to trust God's ultimate desire for Kingdom relationships. Through our journey of discovery, you will be encouraged along your walk to know that you too can experience divine connections, find accountability, friendship, purpose and so much more. Come along with us on this journey. (Meagan Pinkney is a contributing author)

Daily Dose of Declarations

A 365 Day Journey To Help You Declare Positive Affirmations Over Your Life. (Meagan Pinkney is a contributing author)

To book Meagan Pinkney or to purchase products and packages please contact her at:
www.meaganpinkney.com
(539) 302-3848

www.ingramcontent.com/pod-product-compliance
Lightning Source LLC
Chambersburg PA
CBHW070442010526
44118CB00014B/2158